La Constitución

DAVID y PATRICIA ARMENTROUT

Rourke
Publishing LLC
Vero Beach, Florida 32964

DOCUMENTOS QUE FORMARON LA NACIÓN

www.rourkepublishing.com

PHOTO CREDITS: Cover Scene, Page 33 © North Wind Picture Archives.
Cover Document image and Pages 15, 35, 39, 41 Courtesy of the U.S. National
Archives and Records Administration. Pages 42, 43 Courtesy of the U.S. National
Archives and Records Administration and Earl McDonald. Title Page ©
PhotoDisc, Inc. Pages 5, 6, 8, 11, 16, 21, 23, 27, from the Library of Congress.
Page 12 from the Department of the Interior. Pages 18, 19, 22, 25, 29, 30, 36 from
Images of American Political History

Página del título: *El Senado y la Cámara de Representantes se reúnen en el edificio
del Capitolio en Washington, D.C.*

Editor: Frank Sloan

Cover and page design by Nicola Stratford

Library of Congress Cataloging-in-Publication Data

Armentrout, David, 1962-
 [Constitution. Spanish]
 La Constitución / David y Patricia Armentrout.
     p. cm. -- (Documentos que formaron la nación)
 Includes bibliographical references and index.
 ISBN 1-59515-708-5 (paperback)
 1. United States. Constitution--Juvenile literature. 2. United States--Politics and
government--1775-1783--Juvenile literature. 3. United States--Politics and
government--1783-1789--Juvenile literature. 4. Constitutional history--United
States--Juvenile literature. I. Armentrout, Patricia, 1960- II. Title.
 E303.A76 2006
 973.4--dc22
                                        2005022629

Impreso en los Estados Unidos

CG

TABLA DE CONTENÍDOS

LA CONSTITUCIÓN DE LOS ESTADOS UNIDOS

Una constitución es un conjunto de reglas o leyes, que rigen una nación, estado u otro grupo organizado. La Constitución de Estados Unidos es un documento legal que explica claramente las leyes y **principios** según los cuales debe funcionar nuestro gobierno. Describe los poderes del gobierno y los derechos del pueblo. Es uno de los documentos más importantes de la historia norteamericana.

Por más de 200 años, Estados Unidos y su sistema de gobierno han servido como modelo para los amantes de la libertad en todo el mundo. La Constitución, escrita por los Padres Fundadores de Estados Unidos, ha sido usada como guía por naciones en todo el mundo que buscan asegurar sus propias libertades.

Gran parte del plan original para la Constitución fue escrito por James Madison. A veces se le llama el padre de nuestra Constitución.

James Madison fue el cuarto presidente de Estados Unidos.

PRIMEROS ASENTAMIENTOS

Los nativos americanos habían habitado Norteamérica por miles de años antes de ser descubierta por los europeos. Comparativamente la historia de los asentamientos europeos en Norteamérica es realmente bastante corta.

Pero no hay duda de que la llegada de los europeos a Norteamérica cambió para siempre el futuro del mundo.

El asentamiento europeo en Norteamérica fue lento al principio. El viaje de Cristóbal Colón en 1492 dio inicio a una época de grandes exploraciones en Norteamérica. Sin embargo, pasarían más de 100 años antes de que se estableciera un asentamiento permanente en lo que es ahora Estados Unidos. En 1565, los españoles fundaron San Agustín en la Florida. Ésta es la ciudad más antigua habitada sin interrupción en Estados Unidos. El asentamiento inglés permanente más antiguo es Jamestown, en Virginia, establecido en 1607. Los peregrinos no llegaron de Inglaterra hasta 1620, cuando se establecieron en la colonia de Plymouth.

Cristóbal Colón fue un famoso explorador europeo.

Los primeros colonos enfrentaron muchos retos, incluyendo largos y peligrosos viajes por mar, enfermedades, hambrunas y ataques de nativos americanos nada amistosos. Cuando se establecieron asentamientos fuertes que ofrecían protección y hacían más fácil la sobrevivencia, la población europea empezó a crecer.

Entonces, un gran número de colonos comenzó a llegar de Inglaterra, Francia, Holanda, Suecia y Alemania.

Los colonos venían en busca de libertad religiosa, aventuras y oportunidades económicas. Las colonias empezaron a crecer e, incluso, a prosperar. Los poderes europeos vieron el gran potencial del Nuevo Mundo. Los celos y la desconfianza entre los gobiernos europeos condujeron a una competencia por el control de Norteamérica.

Los colonos se preparan a abandonar Inglaterra por el Nuevo Mundo.

LUCHA POR EL CONTROL

Hacia 1680 España ocupaba la Florida, Francia controlaba Canadá (conocida como Nueva Francia) y los británicos mantenían colonias a lo largo de la costa atlántica. Por esa época comenzaron una serie de guerras entre Francia y Gran Bretaña que continuarían intermitentemente por casi 100 años.

Las tribus de nativos americanos fueron forzadas a tomar partido y combatir en muchas batallas, a veces peleando unos contra otros. Las colonias británicas no estaban organizadas y a menudo disputaban entre sí, pero su número les daba una gran ventaja sobre los franceses. En 1689, Nueva Francia tenía una población de aproximadamente 12,000, mientras los colonos ingleses ascendían a más de 200,000.

Durante las guerras franco-indias, Gran Bretaña peleó en muchas batallas como esta por el control de Norteamérica.

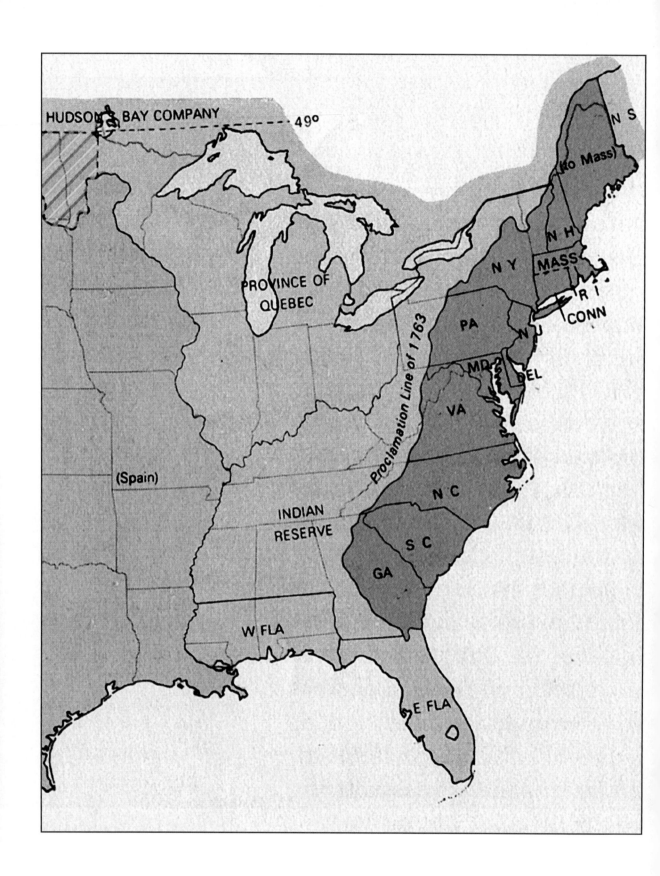

HUDSON BAY COMPANY ····49°

N S

(to Mass)

N H

N Y

MASS

R I

CONN

PROVINCE OF
QUEBEC

PA

N J

Proclamation Line of 1763

MD

DEL

(Spain)

VA

INDIAN
RESERVE

N C

S C

GA

W FLA

E FLA

Las guerras provocaron fuertes pérdidas a todos los involucrados. Francia estaba fatigada por las luchas continuas y buscaba una salida. Finalmente, en 1763, fue alcanzado un acuerdo que dejaba a Gran Bretaña con el control de la mayor parte de Norteamérica. Francia aceptó abandonar sus territorios en Norteamérica. España, que se había aliado con los franceses, fue forzada a ceder la Florida a Gran Bretaña a cambio de La Habana.

Las 13 colonias norteamericanas originales fueron Virginia, Nueva Jersey, Massachusetts, Nueva Hampshire, Pensilvania, Nueva York, Maryland, Connecticut, Rhode Island, Delaware, Carolina del Norte, Carolina del Sur y Georgia.

Un mapa de 1775 que muestra las 13 colonias originales, el territorio británico y el territorio español

EL CAMINO A LA INDEPENDENCIA

Los largos años de lucha y el mantenimiento de las colonias americanas resultaron muy costosos para Gran Bretaña. Cuando la lucha finalmente terminó, Gran Bretaña quedó con una gran deuda. Mientras tanto, las colonias americanas continuaban creciendo a pasos agigantados.

El rey de Inglaterra y el **parlamento** británico buscaron vías para pagar parte de los gastos del mantenimiento de América. El lugar más obvio al que debían mirar era a las propias colonias americanas. Las colonias, razonaban, estaban recibiendo protección de la Madre Patria pero no estaban pagando una parte justa de los costos. Para recaudar dinero, el parlamento británico aprobó una serie de **actas** o leyes a partir de 1764. Las leyes gravaban a las colonias por diversos productos.

Para 1770, la población colonial era de más de 2 millones.

Esta ilustración, publicada en el siglo XVIII, muestra a los ciudadanos de Boston como prisioneros bajo el dominio de Gran Bretaña.

Las nuevas leyes de impuestos no tuvieron popularidad entre los colonos porque los colonos no tenían representación en el parlamento británico. A los colonos les parecía que no tenían derechos legales. Los colonos insistían en que debían ser oídos.

Le dijeron al parlamento que no era justo tener que pagar impuestos sin representación. Al ver que sus quejas fueron ignoradas, muchos colonos comenzaron a organizar protestas. Las protestas provocaron escaramuzas entre los colonos y los soldados británicos.

La ira de los colonos contra Gran Bretaña creció y para 1774 muchos reclamaban la independencia. Lo impensable ocurrió en 1775 cuando estalló la guerra entre las colonias y Gran Bretaña en las batallas de Lexington y Concord.

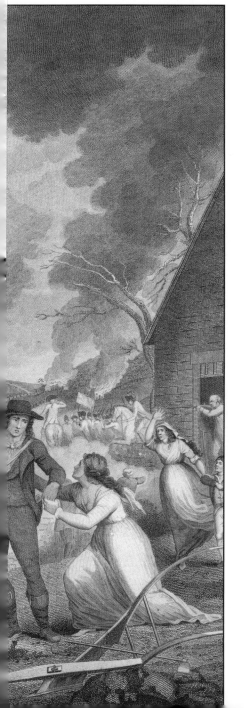

Aunque la libertad se convirtió en la base de la lucha de las colonias por la independencia, la esclavitud era común en muchas de las primeras colonias. Para 1770 sólo en Virginia había más de 187,000 esclavos.

La primera batalla importante de la Guerra de Independencia tuvo lugar en Lexington, Massachusetts, en 1775.

LA DECLARACIÓN DE INDEPENDENCIA

En 1775, un grupo de representantes de las 13 colonias se reunió para decidir qué debía hacerse sobre el conflicto con Gran Bretaña. El grupo, conocido como el Segundo Congreso Continental, incluyó famosos **patriotas** tales como Samuel Adams, Patrick Henry, John Hancock, John Adams, Thomas Jefferson, Benjamin Franklin y George Washington. El Congreso intentó resolver las disputas pacíficamente. Cuando sus esfuerzos fracasaron, el Congreso norteamericano votó a favor de declarar la independencia de Gran Bretaña.

A Thomas Jefferson, conocido por su talento con la palabra escrita, le pidieron que preparara una declaración en la que se anunciara al mundo que las colonias ya no eran parte de Gran Bretaña. En la declaración, Jefferson escribió: *"que estas Colonias Unidas son, y deben serlo por derecho, estados libres e independientes; que quedan libres de toda lealtad a la Corona Británica, y que todo vínculo político entre ellas y el estado de Gran Bretaña queda y debe quedar totalmente disuelto."*

El Congreso Continental aprobó la versión final de la Declaración de Independencia el 4 de julio de 1776.

John Adams fue un miembro del Primer y el Segundo Congreso Continental y fue el segundo presidente de Estados Unidos.

Una de las primeras tareas del Segundo Congreso Continental fue escoger un jefe militar. George Washington fue nombrado comandante en jefe del Ejército Continental y tomó el mando de las fuerzas de las colonias en Boston el 3 de julio de 1775.

Firma de la Declaración de Independencia

¿GUERRA CIVIL?

Muchos de los colonos que todavía no se habían resuelto a favor de la independencia se conmovieron por las palabras de Jefferson. Aunque no todos estaban convencidos de que la independencia era la mejor opción, ahora era muy tarde para retroceder. Los colonos que no querían la independencia y preferían mantenerse bajo el dominio de Gran Bretaña fueron llamados realistas. Los historiadores estiman que de un 20 a un 40 por ciento de la población colonial se mantuvo leal al rey. A veces los miembros de una misma familia tomaban bandos opuestos. Un ejemplo famoso es el de Benjamin Franklin y su hijo, William. Benjamin Franklin se puso de parte de aquellos que querían la independencia, mientras su hijo apoyaba al rey. La lucha entre compatriotas convirtió a la revolución, al menos en parte, en una guerra civil.

Una vez tomada la decisión de lograr la independencia, el Congreso Continental estaba preparado para centrar su atención en hacer la guerra y construir una nueva nación.

Benjamin Franklin (sentado a la izquierda) fue uno de los cinco miembros del que ayudó a escribir la Declaración de Independencia.

LOS ARTÍCULOS DE LA CONFEDERACIÓN

La guerra contra Gran Bretaña consumiría a las colonias durante los próximos años. El Congreso emplería buena parte de su tiempo en encontrar vías de pagarle al nuevo Ejército Continental. Se enviaron **embajadores** a Francia, España, Holanda y a otras naciones buscando ayuda para la lucha en las colonias. Pero muchos miembros del Congreso ya estaban mirando hacia el futuro.

En 1776, Richard Henry Lee, un delegado de Virginia, propuso que el Congreso preparara un acuerdo constitucional formal entre las colonias. El acuerdo fue llamado los Artículos de la Confederación que se convertiría en la primera Constitución de los Estados Unidos. Los Artículos de la Confederación fueron cuidadosamente diseñados para establecer un sistema de gobierno al tiempo que se limitaba el poder de la autoridad federal. El Congreso adoptó los Artículos de la Confederación en 1777. Sin embargo, los Artículos de la Confederación no se hicieron efectivos hasta 1781, cuando el documento fue ratificado oficialmente por todos los 13 estados.

Richard Henry Lee creía que las colonias debían tener una constitución.

ARTICLES

OF

Confederation

AND

Perpetual Union

BETWEEN THE

STATES

OF

New Hampshire, Massachusetts Bay, Rhode Island, and Providence Plantations, Connecticut, New York, New Jersey, Pennsylvania, Delaware, Maryland, Virginia, North Carolina, South Carolina, and Georgia.

WILLIAMSBURG:
Printed by ALEXANDER PURDIE.

Los Artículos de la Confederación fueron la primera Constitución de Estados Unidos de América.

LA GUERRA TERMINA

Después de una guerra larga y sangrienta, Gran Bretaña estaba empezando a mostrar señales de que deseaba una salida. En 1782, los comisionados o representantes de las naciones en guerra se reunieron en París para hablar sobre un acuerdo de paz. Estados Unidos envió a Benjamin Franklin, John Adams y John Jay. Los comisonados firmaron un tratado de paz. Gran Bretaña estuvo de acuerdo en reconocer la independencia de Norteamérica y en retirar las fuerzas británicas del territorio de las colonias.

El tratado fue presentado ante el Congreso estadounidense y ratificado el 15 de abril de 1783, con lo que se terminó oficialmente la guerra.

John Jay ayudó a escribir el acuerdo que oficialmente terminó la guerra con Gran Bretaña.

LA CONVENCIÓN CONSTITUYENTE

No pasó mucho tiempo antes de que las debilidades de los Artículos de la Confederación se hicieran patentes. Los colonos se habían vuelto cautelosos hacia un gobierno central fuerte, bajo el dominio de Gran Bretaña. Los autores de la primera Constitución fueron cuidadosos en limitar el poder del gobierno central. De hecho, los Artículos de la Confederación le daban al Congreso tan poco poder que cualquier ley que éste redactara podía ser, como con frecuencia lo fueron, ignoradas.

Los Artículos de la Confederación trataban a los estados como si fueran países en sí mismos. Los estados estuvieron de acuerdo en que los Artículos de la Confederación no funcionaban. Se necesitaba un gobierno nacional más fuerte. Para hablar sobre los problemas que enfrentaba el Congreso, se convocó a una reunión especial, o convención.

Nuestro gobierno se fundó en la Constitución. Por eso a los autores de este documento se les conoce como los "Padres Fundadores."

George Washington fue electo como presidente de la Convención Constituyente.

La Convención Constituyente se reunió en Filadelfia el 25 de mayo de 1787. El Congreso les había dicho a los delegados a la reunión que consideraran hacer cambios a los Artículos de la Confederación. En lugar de ello, los delegados empezaron a escribir una nueva constitución.

Asistieron a la convención 55 delegados de 12 estados. Muchos de los delegados eran abogados ya familiarizados con la ley y el gobierno. Algunos eran comerciantes exitosos familiarizados con las necesidades de los negocios. Unos pocos poseían fincas y entendían los retos que enfrentaría la gente común. La reunión incluyó a algunos de los hombres más talentosos y más respetados de Norteamérica. Los antecedentes de estos hombres encajaban perfectamente con la tarea que tenían entre manos.

Para septiembre, el **borrador** final del documento ya estaba listo. De los 42 delegados presentes, 39 firmaron con sus nombres aprobando la nueva Constitución. La Constitución fue enviada al Congreso y la reunión de la Convención Constituyente concluyó.

La Constitución fue redactada en el Salón de la Independencia en Filadelfia.

Rhode Island no envió ningún delegado a la Convención Constituyente.

LA NUEVA CONSTITUCIÓN ES RATIFICADA

El Congreso recibió la Constitución a finales de septiembre de 1787. Algunos miembros del Congreso no estaban contentos con que los delegados de la Convención Constituyente hubieran escrito una constitución completamente nueva. Pero como hubo suficiente apoyo a la Constitución, el Congreso estuvo de acuerdo en presentarla a los estados.

Para que la nueva Constitución fuera aprobada era necesario que al menos 9 de las 13 colonias la ratificaran. El 21 de junio de 1788, New Hampshire se convirtió en el noveno estado en ratificar la Constitución y al hacerlo la hizo oficial. El 2 de julio, el Congreso anunció que había una nueva Constitución. Se hicieron planes para un nuevo gobierno en la forma en que era descrito en la Constitución. La ciudad de Nueva York fue nombrada la capital temporal.

El 17 de septiembre es conocido como el Día de la Constitución porque fue el día en que los delegados de la Convención Constituyente se reunieron por última vez para firmar el documento que habían creado.

Firma de la Constitución de Estados Unidos

EL PREÁMBULO

La oración inicial de la Constitución de los Estados Unidos es llamada el preámbulo. El preámbulo explica las razones por las que se formaba un nuevo gobierno:

Nosotros, el pueblo de Estados Unidos, a fin de formar una Unión más perfecta, establecer justicia, asegurar la tranquilidad interior, proveer la defensa común, promover el bienestar general y asegurar para nosotros mismos y para nuestros descendientes los beneficios de la Libertad, establecemos y promulgamos esta Constitución para Estados Unidos de América.

Los autores de la Constitución tenían claro que querían que el pueblo de Estados Unidos disfrutara de justicia, de paz, de la capacidad de defenderse de sus enemigos y de libertad. El gobierno debía trabajar para el pueblo, más bien que lo contrario.

Treinta y nueve delegados firmaron la nueva Constitución.

LOS ARTÍCULOS DE LA CONSTITUCIÓN

La Constitución tiene 4,543 palabras, con los artículos ocupando la sección más grande. Los artículos de la Constitución describen la manera en la cual el gobierno asegurará los objetivos adelantados por el preámbulo. Hay siete artículos en total. Algunos artículos que necesitan explicación adicional están divididos en secciones. Los primeros artículos dividen el gobierno en tres ramas separadas mientras que los últimos cuatro tratan de otros asuntos.

La Constitución crea un sistema de gobierno con "controles y balances." Cada rama del gobierno tiene algún control sobre las decisiones hechas por otra de las ramas. Esto asegura que ninguna rama en particular pueda volverse demasiado poderosa.

La Constitución fue redactada en menos de 100 días.

Artículo I- La rama legislativa

La primera rama del gobierno es la rama legislativa, llamada Congreso. El Congreso está a su vez dividido en dos grupos: la Cámara de Representantes y el Senado. Cada estado tiene representantes en la Cámara de Representantes y en el Senado. Los miembros del Congreso son elegidos por la gente del estado que ellos representan. El Congreso hace las leyes de Estados Unidos.

Artículo II- La rama ejecutiva

La segunda rama es la rama ejecutiva o la presidencia. El presidente debe llevar a efecto las leyes del Congreso. El presidente es además el comandante en jefe de las fuerzas armadas de Estados Unidos.

Artículo III- La rama judicial

La rama judicial del gobierno consiste en el sistema federal de tribunales, incluyendo el Tribunal Supremo. La rama judicial interpreta o explica la Constitución y las leyes del Congreso.

Artículo IV- Los estados

El artículo IV obliga a cada estado a respetar las leyes de todos los otros estados.

El salón de reuniones de la Cámara de Representantes

Artículo V

Los redactores de la Constitución sabían que a medida que los tiempos cambiaran aparecería la necesidad de nuevas leyes. El artículo V explica las reglas que deben seguirse para cambiar o enmendar la Constitución.

Artículo VI - El estatus legal de la Constitución

El artículo VI aclara que la Constitución de Estados Unidos "será la ley suprema del país."

Artículo VII - Ratificación

El artículo final declara que la "nueva" Constitución se haría oficial cuando 9 de los 13 estados la hubieran ratificado o votado en favor de ella.

La edad promedio de los delegados de la Convención Constituyente era de 44 años. Benjamin Franklin era el más viejo con 81 años de edad.

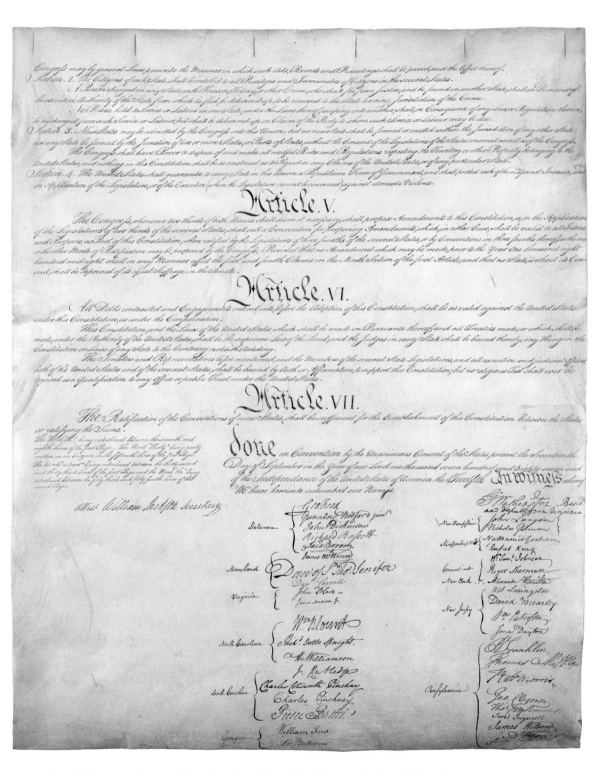

La última página de la Constitución y las firmas de los delegados

ENMÍENDAS

La tinta del pergamino apenas se había secado cuando se propusieron enmiendas a la Constitución. Algunos se quejaban de que la Constitución no ofrecía suficiente protección a los derechos individuales. Bajo las reglas del artículo V de la Constitución, pronto fueron añadidas diez enmiendas. Esas primeras diez enmiendas son llamadas la Declaración de Derechos.

Desde que la Constitución fue **ratificada**, se le han añadido 27 enmiendas al documento. Justo como sus redactores habían previsto mucho tiempo antes, la capacidad de hacer cambios aseguraría que la Constitución siguiera siendo uno de los documentos más importantes de la historia estadounidense.

La Declaración de Derechos está compuesta de las primeras diez enmiendas hechas a la Constitución.

PRESERVANDO LA CONSTITUCIÓN

En julio de 2001 la Constitución de Estados Unidos fue retirada de su exhibición pública como parte de un importante proyecto de restauración llamado Proyecto de Re-encapsulamiento de los Documentos de la Libertad. Los Documentos de la Libertad son la Declaración de Independencia, la Constitución y la Declaración de Derechos.

Los Documentos de la Libertad restaurados están ahora en exhibición pública.

Después de sacar los documentos de sus cajas, los científicos examinaron el estado de la Constitución. Cuidadosamente revisaron cada letra para detectar los daños y limpiaron y le dieron tratamiento al **pergamino**. El Instituto Nacional de Normas y Tecnología construyó cajas especiales para guardar los Documentos de la Libertad. Cinco cajas preservan las cuatro páginas de la Constitución y su página de transmisión firmada por George Washington. Las cajas están llenas con gas argón el cual protege los documentos de daño ambiental. Los Documentos de la Libertad fueron puestos de nuevo en exhibición en los Archivos Nacionales en Washington, D.C. en septiembre de 2003.

Los conservadores revisan cada detalle de la Constitución.

CRONOLOGÍA

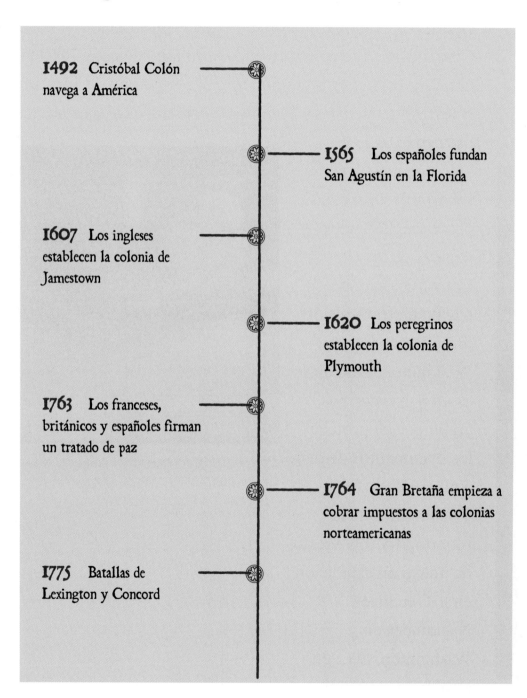

1492 Cristóbal Colón
navega a América

1565 Los españoles fundan
San Agustín en la Florida

1607 Los ingleses
establecen la colonia de
Jamestown

1620 Los peregrinos
establecen la colonia de
Plymouth

1763 Los franceses,
británicos y españoles firman
un tratado de paz

1764 Gran Bretaña empieza a
cobrar impuestos a las colonias
norteamericanas

1775 Batallas de
Lexington y Concord

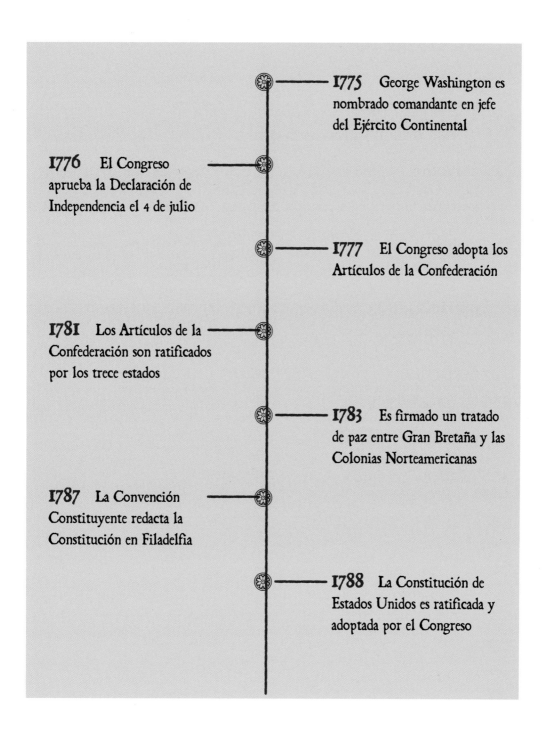

1775 George Washington es nombrado comandante en jefe del Ejército Continental

1776 El Congreso aprueba la Declaración de Independencia el 4 de julio

1777 El Congreso adopta los Artículos de la Confederación

1781 Los Artículos de la Confederación son ratificados por los trece estados

1783 Es firmado un tratado de paz entre Gran Bretaña y las Colonias Norteamericanas

1787 La Convención Constituyente redacta la Constitución en Filadelfia

1788 La Constitución de Estados Unidos es ratificada y adoptada por el Congreso

GLOSARIO

actas — documentos que han sido aprobados formalmente por una organización directriz

borrador — una copia inicial o sin pulir de un documento

embajadores — personas de rango enviadas por un gobierno para representarlo frente a otro gobierno

parlamento — grupo de personas elegidas para hacer leyes

patriotas — personas que aman a su país y están dispuestas a luchar por él

pergamino — papel grueso hecho de la piel de un animal y usado para escribir

principios — verdades, leyes o creencias básicas

ratificado — aprobado oficialmente

LECTURAS RECOMENDADAS

Murray, Stuart. *American Revolution.* DK Publishing, 2002.

Nardo, Don. *The U.S. Constitution.* KidHaven Press, 2002.

Sobel, Syl. *The U.S. Constitution and You.*
    Barron's Educational Series, Inc., 2001.

SITIOS EN LA RED

www.archives.gov/national_archives_experience/constitution.html

www.americanrevwar.homestead.com/files/INDEX2.HTM

www.constitutionfacts.com/

ÍNDICE

HOWELL
Beginner's guide to

Dogs: Their Choice & Care

David Alderton M.A.

Editor
Dennis Kelsey-Wood

HOWELL BOOK HOUSE Inc.
230 Park Avenue
New York, N.Y. 10169

984

Library of Congress Cataloging-in-Publication Data

Alderton, David.
  Howell beginner's guide to dogs.

  Summary: Surveys the world of dogs, including the choice of a puppy, responsible dog ownership, and their care, health matters, and breeds.
  1. Dogs—Juvenile literature. 2. Dog breeds—Juvenile literature. [1. Dogs] I. Title. II. Title: Dogs, their choice and care.
SF426.5.A44   1984   636.7   85-18123
ISBN 0-87605-918-3

Printed in Hong Kong through Bookbuilders Ltd

Photographs © Panther Photographic International 1983

Layout Design by Routedale Ltd, Cornwall, England

Contents

1. Choosing Your Puppy

Dogs were companions to man as long ago as the Bronze Age, before the dawn of modern civilization, with their ancestors being trained to hunt, guard and herd other animals. While dogs still fulfil this working role today, throughout the world millions more are kept simply as pets.

The purchase of a young puppy is a great responsibility, however being an expensive and time-consuming undertaking. Ownership of a dog is still not given enough thought in advance; this is borne out by the fact that millions of dogs are destroyed annually in Britain and the USA alone, the vast majority simply because they were abandoned or are unclaimed strays.

While choosing to take on an adult stray dog can be very worthwhile, it carries many more potential problems for the novice owner than starting with a puppy of one's own choice. The temperament of such a dog is usually unknown, while its past experiences may have made it nervous and most unsuitable for a home where young children are also present. Puppies will not have developed such fears and, with proper training from the outset, should not present the difficulties associated with the acquisition of an older animal.

Tibetan Terrier Puppies

The Choice of a Puppy

A large variety of mongrels, resulting from the unintentional mating of two different pedigree breeds in the first instance, are often available at little or no financial cost. This is not to say that the subsequent cost of keeping such dogs is any less than that of pedigree animals. Indeed, it may even prove to be more expensive because, unless the mongrel's parentage is clearly known, it may well develop into a larger adult dog than was initially hoped.

Size is an important factor when choosing any dog, because a large animal will grow, soon taking over a small apartment, for example; then, if deprived of adequate exercise, it is likely to prove very destructive. A smaller breed is likely to require less exercise, and will be cheaper to feed, as well as being easier to control on a lead. The lifespan of larger breeds is generally several years shorter than that of smaller dogs.

Various breeds are preferred for certain activities, with German Shepherd Dogs and Dobermanns often being trained as guard dogs. Border Collies are well-known for their ability to control sheep while, in Australia, Cattle Dogs (Heelers) or Kelpies perform a similar function but are more aggressive, as their work demands. Gundogs, trained to bring back shot game-birds, for example, include numerous breeds of Retrievers and Spaniels.

If one is aiming to show and subsequently to breed from the puppy, then its initial cost will be that much higher, this reflecting the higher cost of breeding pedigree dogs. It should be pointed out that certain breeds have an increased incidence of particular physical problems associated with them. Entropion, or inturned eyelids, is commonly seen in the Chow Chow, as well as distichiasis, which gives the dog an abnormal set of eye-lashes. Beagles, as another example, are prone to intervertebral disk disorders. Such problems are mentioned later, in various sections, so that the prospective owner can be aware of the potential abnormalities most commonly encountered in different breeds.

The tall and the small in dogs – an Irish Wolfhound towers over his Dachshund friend.

Welsh Corgis are always a popular choice.

The amount of time required for grooming is another point which should be considered when deciding between the various breeds. Smooth-coated dogs, such as Boston Terriers, are much less demanding in this respect than, for example, Poodles, Afghans, or many of the Terriers. These breeds will require periodic trimming or even stripping, certainly for showing, apart from regular daily grooming.

Dog or Bitch

The sex of the puppy is another matter which must be decided upon, preferably before actually obtaining one. As a rule, bitches are more tolerant than dogs, so are better in a home with children, but their two breeding 'heats' each year are a major drawback. Nevertheless, there are various ways of lessening, or overcoming, the difficulties arising from their reproductive cycle, and a veterinarian can advise on this.

If it is hoped to breed from the puppy later on, then of course a bitch should be chosen. Nevertheless, male dogs make excellent companions, so it is really a question of one's personal circumstances. Some males tend to wander more than others in search of females, however, and it is not easy to curb this behavior. In addition, toy dogs are occasionally oversexed, and drag themselves along a carpet, or even attempt to mount suitable objects to overcome their frustration. Such behavior can cause embarrassment in front of visitors, and may be a deterrent for some owners; although, again, a veterinarian can offer help for the problem.

Age of the Puppy

As suggested previously, it is generally preferable to obtain a young puppy, just after weaning, at the age of seven or eight weeks rather than an older youngster. Puppies usually settle in well at this age whereas, later, those which have been living in kennels for longer, are often more nervous and prove harder to house-train successfully. Some breeders, however, will keep puppies in their homes and see them over this preliminary training period – for a fee. Such a service may be advantageous, enabling the dog to be part of a household, so that the subsequent move to a new domestic environment is much less traumatic.

9

2. Points about Purchasing

There are many ways to locate a suitable puppy and many desirable places to find one. Obviously, if you are interested in a popular breed, finding your puppy will be much easier than locating something more unusual or exotic. Newspaper ads, veterinarians, local kennel clubs and dog magazines can direct you. Sometimes asking a person who owns a dog of the breed you want will give good leads to getting your own pet.

Visiting shows is another means of contact, and particularly recommended if one is hoping to obtain a puppy with a view to showing it later. It gives one an opportunity to see, at first hand, what type of dog is required by judges, and the procedure adopted at such events.

Purchasing puppies from reputable pet shops is also recommended, but ensure they have not come from a 'puppy farm', which buys in and then acts as a centre of distribution for dogs of all breeds. This stress of movements, and close contact with other dogs from many backgrounds at an early age, will lead to an increased risk of illness developing in the puppies. Stress is a major predisposing factor in the development of parvovirus infections, which may prove fatal, especially in a young puppy.

That most noble
of breeds –
the Pekingese.

10

What to Look For

Before handling a puppy, the owner's permission should be requested and then, supporting the rear end firmly with a hand or arm, it can be examined more closely. A healthy youngster will be quite plump, with an adequate covering of puppy fat, but a distinct pot-bellied appearance is a sign of poor condition, perhaps caused by intestinal worms. The following points will act as a basic checklist in selecting a healthy puppy:

Look for:	Avoid puppies with:
1. Bright, clear eyes	Dull, weeping eyes
2. Skin being relatively free over the body, full of luster with no signs of lice, fleas, spots or reddening	Tight, dull skin, with signs of parasites in the fur
3. Flattish umbilicus or navel	Any signs of abnormal swelling in this region, which may signify a hernia. Seen quite often in Airedale Terriers
4. Movement without any stiffness	Significant bowing of limbs
5. A lively and playful disposition	Dull and depressed nature, and those carrying their tails between their legs, as this is a sign of a nervous disposition

Whenever possible, by prior arrangement with the owner, one should visit the kennel from whence the puppy is coming. This affords an opportunity to see its surroundings, and select the puppy personally. The mother and, perhaps, the sire will also be on view in most cases. Visits enable one to chat to the breeders, the majority of whom are very ready to advise about the puppy's specific requirements, and discuss points about the breed in general. In this way a great deal of useful information can be gleaned from a specialist breeder.

Questions to Ask

The breeder should be asked for a diet sheet, and the feeding regimen to which the puppy is accustomed. It is also useful to know whether the pup has been wormed and, if possible, which treatment has been used. Any vaccination certificates should also be requested. The appropriate Kennel Club registration, and the pedigree may be available at the time of collection, but often there is a delay in obtaining the registration documents. It is much easier to sort out the relevant paperwork at this stage, however, rather than leaving it until a later date.

The pedigree shows the ancestry of the puppy extending back over four or five generations but is not, in itself, a registration document. The breeder should have registered the litter with the Kennel Club within four weeks of their birth, and may subsequently have named each puppy individually for the register. If this is the case, it will be necessary to complete a transfer form which, with the original registration document, must be sent back to the Kennel Club so that the change of ownership can be recorded. Alternatively, it is simply a matter of selecting a name to accompany the registration form.

Taking the Puppy Home

The puppy should be moved in a snug cardboard box, lined with an old clean towel. This is the safest method, because the young dog will not be used to the unfamiliar sensation of being driven and, as a result, may well be sick. It will, in fact, take a while for the body's senses to become accustomed to this new sensation.

On Arrival Home

Now in a strange environment, away from his fellows, the puppy should be allowed to settle down quietly for a day or so. It is a good idea, on arrival, to offer a milky drink, in which some glucose or honey has been dissolved. Goat's milk is less likely to cause diarrhea than cow's milk, especially if the puppy is not used to the latter. The mixture should be given lukewarm, rather than hot or cold.

The feeding regimen adopted by the breeder should be adhered to, if at all possible, for the first few days, as this will help reduce the risk of digestive disturbances. For the same reason, food containers must always be washed thoroughly after each meal, and a fresh bowl of water given daily.

Veterinary Advice

A visit to the local veterinarian should be made shortly after the puppy's acquisition so that it can be given a check-up, and the necessary vaccinations. Until these take effect, giving satisfactory immunity, it is not advisable to take the puppy out for walks in public places, such as parks, or allow close contact with other dogs. However, this does not mean that the youngster should be kept indoors in complete isolation, because an early period of so-called 'socialization' is important. Given the run of a garden, and taken out for drives, ensures that a puppy's natural curiosity is not stunted, leading to subsequent nervousness.

The veterinarian will be able to advise on the use of dietary supplements, such as calcium and Vitamin D_3 preparations for good bone development. A worming program is another important consideration to be discussed with the Vet, who can prescribe suitable, effective treatments for the various parasitic worm infections which a puppy may encounter. These may well differ according to the region of the world, as discussed later.

3. Responsible Dog Ownership

Regrettably, the population at large contains an increasing proportion of people who dislike dogs and indeed, man's best friend is already the subject of restrictions in certain parks and other public places where dogs are either banned or must be on a lead (leash). The dog owner has a responsibility to the community, as well as to himself and to his pet.

Consideration for Neighbors

If left alone to its own devices, the dog is likely to wander into a road, and could cause an accident for which its owner might well be held responsible. As a precaution, an insurance policy, to cover against claims arising from such accidents, should always be taken out. Some companies offer combined policies, which also include cover for veterinary fees with, of course, some specific limitations and exceptions. Scavenging from rubbish-bins and other refuse sites is likely to result in digestive upsets, quite apart from annoying the neighbors. Sadly today in major cities, there are packs of dogs, including pedigree animals, running wild, which are a constant source of nuisance. An identification disk or similar marking must always be attached to the collar, so that if the dog does accidentally stray, and is then rounded up by the authorities or otherwise caught, tracing its owner will be a straightforward matter.

Neighbors in the immediate vicinity may very easily be affected by the acquisition of a dog, and this can generate ill-feeling if their privacy is subsequently disturbed. A dog should be taught, from the outset, that it will be left alone for short periods and must not bark or howl incessantly when this happens. This is often harder to achieve with an older animal and, in really severe cases, the only way to cope with the difficulty is to obtain tranquillizers from a veterinarian.

There is a noticeable difference between this noise and a definite, purposeful warning bark, serving to alert the dog's owner to the presence of a stranger nearby. Given a suitable introduction, the dog soon becomes familiar with neighbors, and will not bark when it sees them moving about their own property. Firmness in the early period of training will be rewarded subsequently by eliminating such bad traits before they become habitual.

Sometimes it can be difficult to stop a dog straying, especially if there is a bitch on heat in the vicinity, but the provision of secure fencing around a garden will be essential. Although dogs do not climb, German Shepherds, for example, are capable of jumping to a height of 1·8m. (6ft.) without too much difficulty, if they are sufficiently determined. Digging can also provide a way out of a garden so, at first, the dog should, if possible, always be accompanied into the garden or watched closely.

Dogs must *always* be on leads when near, or on, roads.

When being exercised in the country, dogs must always be kept on a lead while in the vicinity of livestock. This is a legal requirement in countries such as Britain, where it is included as a provision of the Wildlife and Countryside Act, 1981. Farmers have a right to shoot dogs which are upsetting, even if not actually harming, their livestock. Dog owners can also be prosecuted for not possessing a licence for their pet. These are renewable annually, being obtained from Post Offices in Britain.

Consideration for the Dog

Dogs, like other animals, appreciate a routine which starts when they are introduced to the family circle. It is preferable to be firm from the beginning, then gradually relent as desired, rather than adopt the reverse approach. It is unfair, for example, to let the sweet little pup sleep on the bed, only to decide, several weeks later, that it is getting too big and should spend the night elsewhere.

Unintentional cruelty can develop into the actual loss of a pet, especially during hot weather. For example, dogs will rapidly become miserable and wander off from a beach while their owners are sun-bathing. If confined to a vehicle, especially one with no ventilation, they are likely to succumb to heat-stroke and die from hyperthermia. Unlike humans, dogs cannot sweat efficiently, but lose excess heat from their bodies by panting. They do possess some sweat glands, however, located between the pads of their feet.

Many dogs find it upsetting to be taken shopping through busy areas, surrounded on all sides by people. Other human activities, such a Bonfire Night or Independence Day Celebrations, can also mean misery for pets, unless they are secured indoors, away from the fireworks. Storms may have a similar effect, with the dog choosing to hide under a chair or somewhere else where it feels secure.

14

Consideration for the Family

With luck, the puppy will be part of the family for more than ten years. It must, therefore, adapt to its environment, while both parties realize what is expected of them. A well-trained dog is a delight for all who come into contact with it. On the other hand, soiled carpets, chewed furniture and scratched doors will result from inadequate training, and lead to family tensions.

Each dog is an individual and, as a member of a family, part of a unique environment. When problems arise, there are various individuals and organizations who can be contacted for advice. Attendance at training classes is especially useful for the novice owner, while additional help can always be sought from veterinarians and from most breeders. In the majority of cases, the owner is usually partially to blame for a behavioral problem, albeit unintentionally, and will need to be guided in order to help the dog. The original choice of breed will affect the degree of difficulty in training one's dog. Working breeds, as well as Gundogs, respond to instruction – it is a vital part of their make-up. Terrier breeds and Hounds have totally different temperaments and their training can prove more difficult.

These American Cocker Spaniels make delightful pets but their coats will need regular grooming.

15

4. Accommodation and Other Needs

From the outset, the puppy should be encouraged to recognize and use its bed. A washable bed is always to be recommended, but it may be worth deferring the decision as to the type until after the teething phase has passed. A cheap, temporary basket can be made by cutting the side out of a suitable cardboard box, and this will be easy to replace if it is chewed or soiled. The bottom of the basket can be lined, using old newspapers, with some clean blanketing or sheets on top for the puppy to lie on; this will also require regular changing. The bed should be placed in a relatively warm position, by a radiator, for example.

At times, it may be necessary to confine the puppy within the room itself, and there are open, wire travelling cages, available as individual panels, which simply clip together, and can also be used for this purpose. After the teething phase has passed, by the age of six months, a permanent basket can be purchased. Circular, wicker dog-baskets are often seen, but metal designs, generally rectangular in shape, allow the dog to stretch out and are probably easier to wash thoroughly. Many dogs enjoy lying and playing on bean bags; this is fine, providing they do not actually destroy the bag, spilling out the contents all over the room.

Other Necessary Items

Stainless steel feeding bowls are preferable to those made of plastic, because they cannot be chewed. Once a plastic bowl is damaged in this way, it becomes much harder to clean thoroughly. The heavier, glazed earthenware bowls are also suitable, with the added advantage over stainless steel that they are less likely to be tipped over, spilling fluid all over the floor.

A collar and lead can be obtained from the outset, although the puppy will not be able to go out safely in public places, until its course of vaccinations is completed when it is about twelve weeks old. Nevertheless, in the interim period, it is useful to get the youngster used to wearing a collar and lead. Only a light collar is required at this stage, being put on just tight enough to prevent it falling off over the head. Simple, stitched designs should be selected for young puppies because, if either item is chewed, and rivets or staples are present, these pieces of metal may be swallowed and could result in subsequent intestinal problems.

Grooming and Bathing

There are various suitable tools for grooming, but a stout brush and comb will be essential. The bristles of the brush should be reasonably firm, so that they do not just slide over the surface of the hair. A metal comb is also preferable, and will serve to remove much of the loose hair. Although dogs lose hair throughout the year, the amount lost is noticeably increased when they are molting properly. Amongst other grooming accessories, a flea comb is a valuable acquisition, while a hound- or grooming-glove is also useful for giving the coat an attractive finish.

Grooming should start from the base of the neck down to the tail, then switch to the flanks and, finally, the legs and head. During a molt, it is worth running a hand through the coat in the opposite direction, to loosen the hair which is then removed by combing. Although bathing is not necessary on a regular weekly basis, there are times when the youngster will benefit from a bath; perhaps to control fleas for example.

The directions for using medicated shampoos must be followed closely, and the preparation kept out of the eyes. The water should be tepid rather than cold and obviously it is preferable to bath the dog outside, if possible, on warm days. Subsequently, it will need to be kept in a similar temperature to dry off, after a brief towelling.

Regular daily grooming is to be recommended, not only to improve the appearance of the coat, but also because it will ensure that the puppy is relatively used to being handled at close quarters, and should not resent it later. Grooming also affords the opportunity to give an overall health check. The ears can be inspected for any signs of infection, the length of the claws noted in case they need cutting, and the mouth can be opened to examine the teeth. Subsequently, either at the Vet's or at home, any treatments required are much more straightforward for the person concerned to administer, and less distressing to the dog.

This elegant Afghan Hound will need a lot of attention.

Toys

While young puppies are very playful by nature, they do not require elaborate toys, which may be easily destroyed with parts being swallowed accidentally. A large ball, which cannot cause harm is ideal; while the 'chews' available from pet stores, help to fulfil this deep-seated desire of all puppies. Only large marrow bones from cattle should be given to dogs; these cannot become stuck in the throat or lower down the digestive tract, and they should not splinter, which can be equally harmful. Dangerous household objects and clothing, such as cotton reels and tights, should always be kept out of reach.

Kennelling

While the majority of people who keep a dog will want it to live in the home, a few prefer, for a variety of reasons, to house their pet in an outdoor kennel. Various companies produce individual kennels, or ranges, which should be sited on well-drained land whenever possible. The shelter part of the kennel must be dry, and draught-proof, as well as being easy to clean. A raised bed, with suitable bedding, will also be needed.

Outdoor runs can have a covering of earth or grass, although these are very difficult to keep clean. Concrete floors can be somewhat hard on the feet, but are easily washed down. Gravel provides quite good drainage, like concrete, but is much harder to clean satisfactorily. The sides of the run should be set into the ground on blocks, to deter any dog from digging its way out, while the roof can be open, or wired over. This will be influenced partly by the height of the structure, which, for convenience of access should ideally be about 1·8m. (6ft.).

The Boston Terrier is compact, neat, and very playful – an ideal companion.

5. Feeding

Dogs are primarily carnivorous in their feeding habits, being dependent on meat as their main source of food. This specialization is reflected in their pattern of dentition, with dogs having teeth adapted for catching and tearing prey, and lacking the prolonged chewing capacity seen in herbivores, such as sheep.

Constituents of Foodstuffs

Apart from water, food is comprised predominantly of proteins, carbohydrates and fats. Each group fulfils specific functions in the body. Protein, for example, is necessary for healthy growth, so a puppy's protein requirement is higher than that of an adult dog. Certain of the individual constituents of proteins, known as amino acids, are essential and cannot be synthesized by the body, so must be present in the diet. Proteins of animal origin are much less deficient in these amino acids than are plant proteins.

Protein can also be used as a source of energy, although this is the main function of carbohydrates. Dog meal and biscuits made from cereals are basic sources of carbohydrate. Fats serve as a much more concentrated form of energy than do carbohydrates; indeed, if there is an imbalance in the dietary intake of carbohydrate compared with energy expenditure, fats can be produced from carbohydrates within the body. As in the case of amino acids, certain fats, such as linoleic acid, are essential, while fat generally serves to make the food more palatable.

Dogs are also known to require a minimum of thirteen vitamins, the majority of which will be obtained from their diet. Vitamins fulfil diverse roles in the body, ranging from assisting in the breakdown of foodstuffs as parts of enzymic systems, to helping to ensure healthy eyesight.

The main vitamins and their prime functions are listed below:

Vitamin	Necessary for:
A	Healthy vision
B group	Metabolic reactions
C	Formation of connective tissue, e.g. wound healing
D	Calcium absorption, mobilization and deposition in the body
E	Fat metabolism
K	Blood clotting

Minerals comprise the other major group of chemicals which must be present in the diet. In the case of a puppy, calcium and phosphorus are most significant, being crucial, along with vitamin D₃, for the development of a healthy bone structure. The ratio between these two minerals should 1·2 : 1, and excessive use of calcium supplements must be avoided because this will upset the ratio. If there is an imbalance with an excess of calcium, for example, then this may be deposited in tissues apart from bone, leading to adverse reactions. Other minerals such as zinc are, like vitamins, important in metabolic reactions. These, being required only in minute quantities, are also known as trace elements.

Feeding Dogs

'Convenience' foods for dogs are now widely available although a varied diet, which includes some fresh meat, is to be recommended. There are many brands of canned foods marketed world-wide, the majority of which are prepared to a very high

Nutrient	Units	Puppy	Adult Dog
Protein	(gm.)	9·6	4·8
Fat		2·2	1·1
Essential fatty acids		0·44	0·22
Minerals:			
Calcium	(mg.)	484	242
Phosphorus		396	198
Sodium chloride		484	242
Potassium		264	132
(Trace elements):			
Magnesium		17·6	8·8
Copper		0·32	0·16
Iron		2·64	1·32
Zinc		4·4	2·2
Manganese		0·22	0·11
Iodine		0·068	0·034
Selenium	(mcg.)	4·84	2·42
Vitamins:			
A	(IU)	220	110
D		22	11
E		2·2	1·1
B Complex–Thiamin	(mcg.)	44	22
Riboflavin		96	48
Pantothenic acid		440	220
Niacin		500	250
Pyridoxine		44	22
Folic acid		8	4
Biotin		4·4	2·2
Vitamin B₁₂		1	0·5
Choline	(mg.)	52	26

standard, and include all the essential nutrients in balanced quantities. The subject of canine nutrition has been extensively studied by the National Research Council of the National Academy of Sciences in America, and their recommendations, published initially in 1974, are given below on the page opposite. These figures are based on a per kg. weight basis so, for example, in the case of a dog weighing 10 kg., they need to be multiplied by a factor of ten to obtain its daily requirements.

Feeding Allowances

The figures given in this section are not absolute, and they will need to be modified in individual cases, depending upon the dog, its environment and the brand of food used. Sufficient milk and water should be poured over the biscuit meal to soften it, especially for younger dogs, and fresh drinking water *must* always be available. Special canned foods for puppies are now produced, and these should be used if possible; bear in mind, however, that the diet ought not to be changed suddenly when the puppy is first acquired. The risk of digestive problems can be lessened by adhering, for these first few days, to the brand of food used by the breeder, and this should be purchased in advance if possible.

Age	Number of	Toy		Small	
(months)	meals per day	Can	Moist food	Can	Moist food
2	4	⅓	62·5gm. (2·5oz)	½-¾	125gm. (5oz)
4	3	⅓-½	125gm. (5oz)	¾	187·5gm. (7·5oz)
6	2	½	187·5gm. (7·5oz)	1	250gm. (10oz)
		e.g. Yorkshire Terrier		e.g. West Highland White Terrier	
		Medium		Large	
2	4	¾	250gm. (10oz)	1	375gm. (15oz)
4	3	1	375gm. (15oz)	1½	500gm. (20oz)
6	2	1½	500gm. (20oz)	2	750gm. (30oz)
Note: Quantities given are per day, NOT per meal.		e.g. Cocker Spaniel		e.g. German Shepherd Dog	

Figures based on manufacturer's instructions. Imperial conversions are approximate. Biscuit meal is given on an approximately equal volume basis with canned food from four months of age. Prior to this, slightly less biscuit is given. The directions on the packaging of an individual product should be read before use, however, and followed accordingly.

The tables also show that, as the puppy grows into an adult dog, its feeding requirements are bound to change, depending partly on the work it is expected to perform. The adult dog only requires half the protein intake necessary to sustain it, compared with that needed during its growth phase.

In the case of canned foods, some are too rich for a few individuals, and it may be necessary to change to another brand. Nevertheless, such cans, prepared to exacting standards, provide an economical way of keeping a dog in good condition. Some biscuit meal should also be offered, with brands containing yeast proving most palatable. The meal is a major source of carbohydrate and, if the dog appears to be getting overweight, the amount of meal in the diet should be reduced.

In addition, there are now various dry and semi-moist products produced for dogs. These must always be fed in accordance with the manufacturer's instructions, as they may otherwise prove harmful. With regard to fresh meat, beef, horsemeat and other items are commonly used as dog food but, unlike most commercially-prepared foods, these are not in themselves complete diets.

From any standpoint the Great Dane is one big dog. You will need a good bank balance to keep him in food!

6. Training and Exercise

Training a young puppy to fit into a domestic environment is not a difficult procedure, merely a question of routine, coupled with firmness and understanding on the part of the owner. Many towns have organized dog training classes, which meet regularly, and serve to assist both owners and their charges with the basic procedures of obedience training.

House Training

This must be the first lesson mastered by all puppies. Contrary to what might sometimes be thought, dogs are not generally dirty creatures by nature, but puppies need to be taught where they can attend to their natural functions. A puppy will soon respond to being placed outside, when it appears to want to defaecate or urinate. In

The Beagle is almost the perfect family dog but he will require plenty of exercise. They are a 'no frills' breed that can be highly recommended.

the first instance, provision of a low-sided box, lined with newspaper and filled with sand or a similar absorbent substance, will serve as a dirt box. This must be changed as soon as possible after it has been used.

Feeding will usually be followed by bowel movement, and a young puppy may naturally go perhaps six times a day, and urinate even more frequently. This also often happens when the pup wakes up after a snooze.

It is pointless to scold a puppy which has not used its box. Instead, the young dog should be placed outdoors for a brief period, although it is preferable to anticipate the need before it arises. Puppies soon learn to ask to go out when necessary. At night, it is perhaps most effective to have the puppy in the bedroom, and then put the youngster outdoors directly it appears distressed. Failing this, it should be left, with its box standing on a thick layer of newspapers.

Puppies can often be encouraged to use a dirt box, by sprinkling some drops of a preparation available from pet stores which has a suitable scent. It is also important to clean up thoroughly after an accident, using disinfectant, because the puppy may otherwise be tempted, by the scent, to return to this area, quite apart from protecting human health. Conversely, other preparations can be obtained to deter dogs from fouling in a specific place.

Obedience Training

The tone of voice is one of the most potent tools in the trainer's repertoire, and the puppy will soon learn to distinguish between a harsh voice, and a more favorable tone. Firmness and patience, rather than force, will yield the best results. It is important not to confuse the young dog; for example, when the puppy is using a dirt box, praising it while walking away, may result in a following trail over the carpet. A harsh scolding under such circumstances is unjustified.

Obedience training should begin early in the puppy's new life, so that a basic routine is established from the outset. If the dog is not going to be allowed on to chairs or other furniture, it is much easier, and fairer, to make this clear from the beginning by use of the word 'no', and putting the pup back on the floor. A similar approach should be used to stop the dog jumping up at people, as this can be very disconcerting, and potentially dangerous. The two simple commands which must be mastered, initially, are 'stay' and 'sit'. With guidance, these are not difficult for the dog to learn. Placing the puppy in its bed, after feeding or exercise (when it should want to sleep) and repeating 'stay' until the command is obeyed, will soon result in this order being recognized.

Teaching the puppy to sit can be carried out with the 'stay' routine. At first, it may be necessary to apply gentle pressure to the dog's hind quarters to achieve the required posture. This should be repeated at every opportunity, such as before putting down a bowl of food. The puppy can be rewarded with a small tit-bit for responding to a command, but never deprived of its food if it fails to obey, as this will only encourage thieving and related problems.

Once the command 'stay' is mastered, it is possible to teach the puppy to 'come', especially by adding its name to this latter command. Mealtimes can be a useful adjunct to this phase of training, as the puppy soon associates something pleasurable with being called by its name. Having learned to sit, the youngster can then be taught

24

The Border Collie is a 'natural' shepherding breed that responds easily to obedience training. They need to keep busy – and thrive on it. Not a dog for the stay at homes!

the 'down' position. However, this may prove a more difficult task because, being such active creatures, puppies will rarely adopt this position naturally for very long. As a first step, it is often necessary to place them gently on all fours, and get them to 'stay', before they actually grasp the command of 'down'.

As with all lessons, wherever possible, these commands should be taught initially in a confined space, such as a garden, and well away from roads. It is a matter of building up the commands gradually, and repeating those already learned, in conjunction with new ones, as far as possible. In the case of learning to retrieve and drop a ball, for example, the young dog can go from a sitting position to 'come', bringing the ball back, 'drop', and 'down'. In this sequence, the new command is 'drop', the remainder having been learned previously. A dog must be taught to 'drop' early on, so that it does not become difficult to handle in this respect. Encouraging a dog to chase and return with a ball is a useful means of exercizing it, without making too much of a physical demand on its owner. The dog will use up more energy in this relatively short space of time and distance and so not need to be walked so far. More detail of specific exercise requirements is given later, when discussing the various breeds.

The Big Outdoors

A fully grown large dog weighing perhaps 45 kg. (100 lbs) will prove a distinct liability on a lead if it is not used to walking correctly. Therefore, training should begin in the garden, with sessions lasting for a maximum of ten minutes each day, even before all vaccinations have been completed.

The puppy should be walked up and down, on the lead, at first, preferably sandwiched between a wall or fence and its owner, so that it cannot pull away. If the youngster starts pulling ahead, the command 'heel' should be given, and the puppy encouraged to adopt the desired position, using a choke chain if necessary. If the young dog starts dragging behind, a gentle pull on the lead, with words of encouragement, should see the problem overcome. The 'sitting' routine can also be developed in conjunction with lead walking.

Always remember that, no matter how well trained, a dog should *never* be exercised off the lead near to roads as the unforeseen can always happen with, possibly, tragic results. It just is not worth the risk.

When the puppy is taken out, these procedures should be repeated, in the face of distractions such as other pedestrians and traffic. Nevertheless, a young dog must not be over-exercised, particularly at first, and regular daily walks are much better than one long marathon each week-end. In an urban environment, dogs should never be allowed to foul the pavement, and must be taught to use the gutter.

An Old English Sheepdog puppy being taught the 'sit and stay' command – it could save his life one day.

7. Health Matters

This section is not intended to act as a replacement for veterinary advice, which should always be sought whenever a dog appears unwell. Veterinarians can prescribe antibiotics and other modern drugs to maximize the chances of a successful recovery. In addition, with the advent of effective vaccines, diseases such as distemper, which were formerly common killers, are now rarely encountered.

Bleeding

Applying pressure to the site which is bleeding, using a wet cotton-wool pad, is an effective means of stemming even severe blood loss. Minor wounds will respond to being bathed with a solution of potash alum, or even a styptic pencil. If there is a risk of infection or prolonged hemorrhage, especially with a deep wound, then a vet should be consulted.

Claws

Occasionally, these may need to be cut back, especially if the dog has no access to hard surfaces. It is not easy to spot the 'quick' or blood supply of the claws and, as they are very tough, the vet or a groomer can show you how it's done.

Dew claws can be a problem if they were not removed at an early age, as the puppy may subsequently catch and tear one in something. It is, however, possible to remove them later, but this is a more difficult procedure.

Coughing

There are various causes of this complaint, and 'Kennel cough' is, regrettably, common after the dog has come out of boarding kennels. There is now a vaccine against *Bordetella bronchoseptica*, one of the main bacteria causing the infection. It is not generally a serious problem though; but, if there is a physical obstruction causing a cough, such as a bone stuck in the throat, veterinary attention should be sought at once.

Diarrhea

Diarrhea is again a symptom of a disease, rather than a disease itself. Various infections may be implicated as the cause. In the case of parvovirus infection, the feces are often blood-stained. The accompanying loss of fluid will soon result in severe circulatory disorders if left untreated, and will rapidly prove fatal. Therefore, veterinary advice must be obtained, particularly if the pup appears depressed. It is not fair to leave it, hoping that the diarrhea will simply stop; although a puppy's motions can vary considerably in consistency.

Fleas

These parasites are a common problem, especially during the warmer months of the year. They feed on the dog's blood, causing irritation and resultant bouts of scratching and exposure may lead to an allergy developing against the flea's saliva. It is possible to detect these parasites in the fur by means of a fine metal flea-comb, sold by many pet stores. Adult fleas, or more commonly their dirt, visible as black specks, can be seen when the comb, with its hair load, is examined against a white background. Any fleas should immediately be put in water, or 'popped' firmly between the fingernails to prevent them from escaping.

Treatment obtained from a pet shop may be in the form of a powder, aerosol spray or a wash which will also kill lice. Although some of these preparations possess a slight residual insecticidal action, flea collars and medallions are effective over a much longer period. To avoid unpleasant side-effects, they must be used as directed.

Fleas also live and breed in the dog's immediate surroundings, so its sleeping quarters must also be treated, to prevent re-infection. Cats, as well as hedgehogs, can spread fleas to dogs; but, if a cat is also found to be infected, care should be taken over the treatment used, because not all are safe for use on felines.

Hip Dysplasia

The German Shepherd Dog, and other large breeds especially, can suffer from this complaint. The hip joint is, effectively, a ball and socket structure, with the head of the femur normally fitting snugly into the cup of the acetabulum on the hip. Various factors, such as an abnormally shallow acetabulum, will affect this structural arrangement and serve to weaken the joint.

Although pups may appear normal at birth, symptoms can become evident as soon as five months later, and are usually manifested by pain in the affected joints. The hips themselves are not fully developed at this stage, with areas of cartilage still to be replaced by bone, so a variable degree of malformation may occur. Indeed, not all dogs are affected as severely as others.

Various schemes are now operating to detect cases of hip dysplasia, prior to breeding, as the problem can be inherited and it is worth finding out the status of breeding stock when purchasing a puppy. It can be confirmed by radiography, preferably at between two and two and a half years of age. Positioning of the legs is crucial in obtaining a reliable X-ray picture, so some form of anesthetic may be required.

Rabies

This dreaded viral disease can affect all mammals, and not just dogs; although, if infected, they, by virtue of their close contact, then represent a considerable hazard to human health. The virus is endemic in the fox population of parts of Europe and also in the wildlife of areas of North America.

Rabies is not presently found in Britain or Australia, and there are strict quarantine regulations to ensure that the infection does not gain access to these countries.

Information about the movement of dogs should be sought from the appropriate agricultural department of the country concerned, well in advance of the proposed date of import or export.

Vaccinations

These usually offer protection against distemper and canine hepatitis, caused by viruses, as well as leptospirosis which results from a bacterial infection. All these diseases can prove fatal, so it is sensible to take advantage of the protection provided by vaccination, and maintained by 'boosters' which are usually required annually. The vaccines are normally prepared as a combined dose and given together, rather than as three separate injections. Serious side-effects are very rarely encountered; but, if the puppy has been 'off-color' just beforehand, the veterinarian must be informed, because the vaccination, if given then, could possibly prove harmful. A vaccine to protect against parvovirus, which has caused epidemics of disease in many countries recently, is also now recommended by many veterinarians, especially for younger dogs.

Worms

The common types of worms encountered in dogs, especially young animals, are roundworms and tapeworms. The roundworm species *Toxocara canis* is potentially one of the most serious, because it can infect children, and may cause blindness but, thankfully, such occurrences are rare.

Infection passes from the bitch to her developing puppies, which are born with the worms in their intestines. Therefore, they should have been treated from the age of a fortnight onwards, as should the bitch. At this stage, the worms will not have matured sufficiently to pass eggs so, it is hoped, the hazard of human infection will be much lessened if they are eliminated before they can reproduce. Cleanliness is essential, as the eggs will survive in dirty surroundings. As additional precautions, the wearing of gloves when cleaning up, and supervizing contact between children and puppies, as well as thorough hand-washing afterwards, are to be recommended.

Fleas act as intermediate hosts for one of the most common genera of tapeworm, *Dipylidium*, so control of both parasites is required to break the cycle of this infection. Dogs can also become infected from eating the flesh of herbivores which contain intermediate stages of the tapeworm. Treatment, as for roundworms, is by means of a worming dose given in tablet form. Extremely effective remedies are now available from veterinarians.

In some areas of the world, including parts of America and Australia, heartworms are a significant threat to a dog's health. They can live for years in the right ventricle of the heart and adjacent regions of the circulatory system. The intermediate stages, known as microfilariae, are transmitted, from one dog to another, by biting insects such as mosquitoes. It is very difficult to treat this infection, but it can be prevented by giving appropriate medication on a regular basis.

8. Breeds of Dog
by Dennis Kelsey-Wood

It is vital to select a breed which is suitable for the circumstances and environment of its owner and the immediate family. Certain breeds, regrettably, become fashionable simply because they win a major show such as Crufts or Westminster; again, others do so because they are featured in national advertizing campaigns, or star in TV shows. A dog should never be purchased simply on the grounds of its appearance, as this can be very misleading. The Old English Sheepdog seen on the TV or the Afghan magnificently strolling around a show ring may look appealing, which they are, but the amount of care and time that has been spent on preparing the coat for such occasions is far in excess of that which the average family are prepared to devote; therefore, this factor *must* weigh heavily in the choice of breed. Before purchasing, the prospective buyer is well advised not only to consult specialist breed books for more information, but also to contact one or more breeders – who will be happy to advise the extent of work or costs in the breed under consideration. The well known adage 'buy in haste, repent at leisure' was never more apt than when purchasing a puppy.

Siberian
Husky

Division of Breeds

For exhibition purposes the hundreds of known breeds are divided into groups based on the role for which they were originally developed. In the UK these groups are Hounds, Terriers, Working, Toy, Gundog and Utility: in the USA the latter two groups are called the Sporting and Non-Sporting Groups and breeds working with livestock form the Herding group. Australia, with slight variations, has adopted the UK classification.

Within this chapter the breeds are grouped according to their size – a factor which will no doubt greatly influence a prospective owner's choice. The groupings of large, medium and small is not without its problems as clearly certain breeds could be considered as, for example, being medium-sized by one person and large by another. Size, in itself, is not indicative of likely upkeep costs as the Bassett Hound is really a large dog on little legs; therefore, average weights may indicate likely appetites. Weights and heights quoted are average for a male – females will normally be somewhat smaller and lighter. Grooming costs can also add to the upkeep, so reference to these is made where applicable. Space restricts coverage of all but a sampling of popular breeds plus others which are typical of breed groups and, in order to overcome this wherever possible, alternatives are given; these should be the subject of further reference by intending purchasers who may otherwise not be aware of them. Country of origin is given after the name of the breed.

LARGE BREEDS

Afghan Hound   Afghanistan   71 cm. (28 in.)   29·4 kg. (65 lbs)

This elegant hound has the aristocratic looks to match its ancestry. Developed to hunt gazelle, as well as small game, the breed sports a long silky coat which further adds to the 'desert sheik' image. Afghans are deeply suspicious of strangers, are not easily trained and require considerable exercise – apart from the time needed to keep their coat from matting. They are fastidious eaters, consuming less than many much smaller breeds. If you are a novice dog owner then admire them rather than buy them. The experienced dog owner will find them a challenge and thus very rewarding. Similar but with a short coat is the Saluki: other 'racy' breeds are the Borzoi, Greyhound and Scottish Deerhound.

Alaskan Malamute   USA   63·5 cm. (25 in.)   38·6 kg. (85 lbs)

Developed by the Mahlemut tribe as an all-round sled, pack, hunter and guard-dog, this breed is typical of the Spitz group of northern sled dogs. They are courageous, hardy and loyal to their owner. Powerful and strong-willed, they will require firm handling when young lest they 'take over'. Regular grooming of the dense coat is essential. Smaller, but with the same sterling qualities are the pure white Samoyed, the Eskimo Dog, Siberian Husky, Keeshond and Finnish Spitz. The diminutive Pomeranian, at around four and a half pounds, is 'custom made' for Spitz loving apartment dwellers.

Airedale Terrier   England   61 cm. (24 in.)   25 kg. (50 lbs)

The largest of the Terriers, this black and tan breed was, until the spread of the German Shepherd and Dobermann, a very popular choice as guard/police dog. Originally developed near the Wharfe and Aire rivers of Yorkshire as an otter hunter, Airedales make excellent companions and are quite safe with children, easily trained and moderate in their food requirement. However, the coat requires regular stripping which, if done by professionals, will add to the upkeep. Less aggressive than their smaller cousins, they are strong dogs. Similar, but smaller, alternatives are the Lakeland, Welsh, Irish and Wire-haired Fox Terriers – the latter having large white areas of coat.

Boxer   Germany   58·4 cm. (23 in.)   31·8 kg. (70 lbs)

Developed by crossing bull-bating *Bullenbeissers* with Bulldogs, the Boxer has become globally popular as a guard and companion. They are very lively dogs and, like all Bull breeds, hardy and trustworthy – even with the smallest of children. However, compared with other breeds, they do suffer from a high incidence of tumours in later life and, like most Bull breeds with reduced muzzles, can suffer in later life with respiratory problems so their weight must be carefully watched. These problems aside, they make excellent family dogs having a short, minimal grooming, coat and moderate appetites. Pure whites or blacks should be avoided. Alternatives are the heavier Mastiffs and Bull Mastiffs or the lighter and smaller French Bulldog or the Boston Terrier.

Dobermann Pinscher   Germany   68·6 cm. (27 in.)   31·8 kg. (70 lbs)

This black and tan breed was developed by crossing numerous breeds including the Manchester Terrier, German Pinscher and Rottweiler in order to produce a sharp, terrier-like breed that was, however, large enough to be a formidable foe. Ferocity was essential and Louis Dobermann, the German dog catcher for whom the breed was named, succeeded in every way. Whilst, in recent years, breeders have endeavoured to instil reliable temperament into the breed, it has to be stated that

Dobermann
Pinscher

Alaskan
Malamute

It is essential that all
Working breeds, such as
these two, are given both
mental and physical
exercise – if not, then
canine delinquents will
result.

German Shepherd

novice owners should consider very carefully the original role of the breed before purchasing. In the wrong hands they are akin to cocked pistols. Firm but fair training of the dog is absolutely essential if you are not to be the most disliked person in the area! Grooming is minimal. Obvious alternatives would be the heavier Rottweiler, or, for those requiring similar boldness but in diminutive form, the Miniature Pinscher or the Manchester Terrier.

German Shepherd Dog (GSD)   Germany   63·5cm. (25in.)   36·4kg. (80lbs)

The most popular breed of dog in the world, the German Shepherd Dog, or Alsatian as it is still widely known in the UK, has everything going for it and is arguably the most 'complete' breed ever developed by man. Good looks, manageable coat, agility, power and speed all help to make it the all-rounder *par excellence*. Shepherd dog, tracker, rescue dog, guard, guide-dog – you name it – and the GSD can do it. All this in spite of the fact that it has received more adverse press coverage than any other breed. This stated, selection of well bred stock is essential and it is better to pay a little more from a reputable breeder than acquire the 'unknown temperament' of casual backstreet breeders. Early firm training is, as in the Dobermann, essential. Although excellent family dogs, previous dog owning experience is recommended before purchasing the GSD. Whites and long-coated specimens are undesirable. Similar breeds are the Belgian Sheepdog (Groenendael), Malinois and Tervueren.

German Short-haired Pointer

Irish Setter

German Short-haired Pointer (GSP) Germany 61 cm. (24 in.) 29·5 kg. (65 lbs)

Possibly the best all-round sports dog, the GSP was bred for versatility and, no doubt, this accounts for its steady increase in numbers. By crossing original German hounds with Foxhounds, Bloodhounds, Spanish and English Pointers, produced a breed that is ideal for the person who wants a companion, guard and hunter-gundog. As happy in the home as in the field, the GSP requires minimal grooming and sports a docked tail. They are seen at their best in countryside homes where greater opportunity is afforded them to keep fit and exercise their scenting ability. Color can be any combination of liver, liver-roan or liver and white. Alternative possibilities would be the Weimaraner, Vizsla or English Pointer.

Great Dane Germany 81·3 cm. (32 in.) 56·8 kg. (125 lbs)

This breed was developed around 1800, though similar dogs were known to the Greeks and Romans who used them for Boar hunting, guarding and fighting in arenas. Their large size and strength makes them totally unsuitable for confined surroundings. Grooming is minimal but food bill will be high. Whilst affectionate with children their size must again be considered a limiting factor in family homes. Various color shades are available including a harlequin variety. Obvious alternative would be the Irish Wolfhound.

Great Dane

Irish Setter   Ireland   68·6cm. (27in.)   31·8kg. (70lbs)

With its striking rich mahogany red and silky coat, this elegant gun-dog is justifiably popular. Also known as the Red Setter, its cheeky and happy-go-lucky character is well suited to its Irish origins. Very active dogs, they need firm handling when young but will then reward with affection and loyalty. Excellent with children, they are not overly big eaters and require only minimal, though regular, grooming. Not quite as popular, though with great character, is the English Setter which will need a little more grooming as will the other Setter, the Gordon.

Irish Wolfhound   Ireland   81·3cm. (32in. min.)   54·6kg. (120lbs min.)

The tallest dog in the world, the Irish Wolfhound, nearly became extinct before Capt. G. A. Graham, in 1862, began a twenty year revival program on the breed. It is fortunate for us that he succeeded in saving what must be one of the world's truly great breeds. This rough-haired hound was known to the Romans for its ferocity and was eagerly sought by medieval royalty who used it for hunting deer, wolf and the giant elk. In spite of its size and strength, the breed is famed for its gentle disposition which, if space and money permits, make it an excellent family dog. Grooming is minimal, though needed regularly. It may be fawn, brindle, black or cream though usually it will be gray. The smaller Scottish Deerhound is the nearest alternative.

Boxer

Irish Wolfhound

Labrador Retriever   England   58·4cm. (23in.)   30·9kg. (68lbs)

Developed from the lesser Newfoundland, as were many of the Retriever breeds, and used by the fisherman to help in the arduous waters off the Labrador coast, the breed was refined when it arrived, via Poole, into the UK. Now a regular 'top ten' breed on both sides of the Atlantic, the Labrador is a compact, well muscled gun-dog that has turned its talents to many new roles and is seen as guide-dog, tracker, mine and drug detector and is also a useful guard-dog. Its short coat, which may be yellow, black or chocolate, requires minimal grooming and the breed has no physical drawbacks which, allied to its excellent nature, make it a first class family dog. A tendency to put on excess weight needs to be kept in check. There are many alternative choices in Retrievers, these notably being the Golden, with longer hair, the less seen Flat-coated – also sporting long hair, the unusual Curley-coated, or the Chesapeake Bay Retriever. All have the same excellent character and versatility.

Old English Sheepdogs (OES)   England   61cm. (24in.)   27·3kg. (60lbs)

Also known as the Bobtail, the OES is a shaggy looking breed developed for sheep driving in the west country. It is very friendly, highly trainable – though very boisterous – and makes an ideal family dog. However, its profuse coat will take considerable time to groom and, in wet weather, this may create further problems in the home, so only think of this breed if the family is prepared to put up with some inconvenience. Less popular, and with a long coat, is the Bearded Collie – a possible alternative.

Rottweiler

Rottweiler   Germany   66 cm. (26 in.)   43·2 kg. (95 lbs)

This black and tan powerhouse is used extensively as a police and army dog in its homeland – and is gaining in popularity all over the world. Short-haired, therefore requiring minimal grooming, it is often confused by the layman for a Dobermann, in whose development it played a part. Originally, the breed accompanied the Roman legions in their march through Europe and was used to drive and protect cattle. Later, it was used as a draught animal by butchers. Whilst heavy, it is surprisingly agile and very muscular. Although it is less volatile than its obvious competitors in the guard dog stakes – the GSD and Dobermann – it is none-the-less very strong-willed and needs firm control from an early age. Bold and courageous in the extreme, it needs considerable affection and must not be kenneled in isolation. Being stronger than its rivals, the breed's popularity must be a source of mixed blessing; the novice dog owner is not recommended to undertake the breed as a 'first' dog.

Saint Bernard   Switzerland   73·7 cm. (29 in.)   81·8 kg. (180 lbs)

Everyone will know of this breed – such is its fame. The breed's characteristic expression, size and exploits have endeared it to millions over the years. Originally smooth-coated, gene infusions from crossing with the then larger Newfoundland produced the rough-haired variety which is now, almost globaly, seen. Whilst obviously excellent family pets, being gentle and docile, safe even with the smallest of children, their purchase should be the source of considerable deliberation. The dense coat will take time to groom, the appetite is enormous – and costly, whilst the massive bulk of the breed cannot be overlooked. They are not over-active but need good, regular exercise. Alternatives: the Pyrenean Mountain Dog or the smaller, but still substantial Newfoundland, Bernese Mountain Dog and Appenzell Mountain Dog.

MEDIUM SIZED BREEDS

Basset Hound France 35·7cm. (14in.) 20·5kg. (45lbs)

Believed to be the result of crosses between the various French and Belgian Blood-hounds, the Basset is known under numerous names in Europe and numerous varieties exist. The popular Basset of England and the USA is short-coated, requiring minimal grooming. His long ears, doleful expression and short, crooked, legs make him an amusing sight. In reality, he is a full sized dog lacking leg-length. Bassets are very amiable by nature, easy going to the point they are difficult to train, and possessing scenting powers surpassed only by the Bloodhound. They have voracious appetites when young, which belies their small size. Ideal dogs for beginners and for families. Alternative possibility would be the Dachshund.

Basset Hound Puppies

Beagle England 36·8 cm. (14·5 in.) 12·7 kg. (28 lbs)

Possibly the best all-round pet or family dog, having few, if any, drawbacks. Developed to hunt hares, the Beagle is a pack hound and this fact enables him to fit into a family situation with no problems. Short-coated, grooming is thus minimal. Totally reliable by nature, he is not too big to be a problem, nor too small to need pampering. His appetite, for his size, is healthy without being excessive. He has no loose folds of skin or any form of exaggeration which might be the source of health problems. The only cautionary words would be that he will need training not to bay whilst the family is out and may tend to wander if left to his own devices – this is no more than the hunting hound coming out. His diet will need watching and Beagles do need good exercise to keep them from getting overweight. Alternatives – very different, but similar in being ideal pets, are the Manchester Terrier and the Smooth-coated Fox Terrier.

Bull Terrier, Staffordshire England 38·1 cm. (15 in.) 15 kg. (33 lbs)

One of the two true 'fighting' dogs of England, the Staffordshire Bull Terrier has a bloodthirsty heritage. Developed to fight to the death, this little Terrier is probably the toughest dog, pound for pound, in the world – more than a match for dogs considerably larger. With no loose skin, and short hair, grooming is minimal – more a polish than a groom. Solid as a rock, the Stafford is totally dependable around children and therefore an ideal family pet. His drawback lies in his ancestry – he needs no excuse for a fight! Once started he can be difficult to stop – this can give him, and his owner, a bad reputation with other dog, and cat, owners. Kept in check, he is a marvellous family dog who will readily die in your defense. The same can be said for his larger cousin, the Bull Terrier. Both varieties are surprisingly economical to feed. Not the easiest dogs to train, Bull Terriers need careful watching as they seem impervious to both pain and potential dangers.

Chow Chow China 45·7 cm. (18 in. min.) 22·8 kg. (50 lbs)

Known also as the Canton Dog and the Edible Dog, the Chow Chow is unique in that it has a blue-black tongue. Its stilted leg action is likewise a characteristic feature. Normally a red color, there are also black and blue specimens seen. The coat is harsh and dense befitting a member of the Spitz group of breeds. Originally bred as a hunting dog, it is deeply suspicious of strangers, not giving its affections lightly. Excessive facial folds may be the source of problems, especially in later life, whilst the dense coat will need constant grooming. A smooth-coated variety is available, though rare. Whilst they can be excellent family dogs, they are not recommended for the average novice or family looking for a trouble-free pet. Alternatives would be the Samoyed, Husky, Keeshond or the diminutive Pomeranian.

Cocker Spaniel England 39·4 cm. (15·5 in.) 13·6 kg. (30 lbs)

These delightful dogs have enjoyed popularity over many years. Developed to flush birds, especially the Woodcock (for whom the breed is named), Cockers are merry, happy little dogs with short, docked tails. Their singular drawback lies in the grooming and trimming needed to maintain the coat and, in particular, the long pendulous ears which are prone to internal bacterial and mite infections. Good natured, they mix well with family and other animals and have moderate appetites. In the USA the

Bull Terrier

Chow Chow

American Cocker has become very popular and is totally distinct from the English, from which it was developed. Its coat furnishings are extensive and the foreface is somewhat dished. There are numerous alternative Spaniels such as the heavy Clumber, the sprightly Welsh and English Springers, the rare Sussex, the unusual Irish Water Spaniel, the Field and the Brittany – the latter quite popular in the USA.

Fox Terrier, Wire-haired England 39·4cm. (15·5in.) 8·2kg. (18lbs)

Once the most popular pet breed, the Fox Terrier has declined in recent years with the trend towards either large, unusual or toy breeds. However, the breed remains very popular with show-goers. Correctly trimmed, the Wire-haired is an impressive Terrier, being smart, very alert and active: these qualities, combined with his moderate upkeep costs will no doubt, one day, bring him to the fore again. The Smooth-haired variety, not quite as glamorous, has the advantage of needing minimal grooming and, like the Beagle, is in many ways the perfect family pet breed. A miniature variety of the Smooth is known in the USA as the Amertoy. Similar breeds are the Lakeland, Welsh and Irish Terriers, with the Airedale being a giant alternative.

41

Poodle (Toy)

Cavalier King
Charles Spaniel

Poodle, Miniature France/Germany 33 cm. (13 in.) 3·6 kg. (8 lbs)

Known in its countries of origin as *Caniche* and *Pudle*, the breed comes in three distinct sizes – the Standard, Miniature and Toy. Other than this they are identical. Originally, the Standard Poodle was bred as a gun-dog, at which it remains excellent. The breed is highly intelligent, robust and full of life. Master of tricks and always ready for a game, it is not surprising that its rise to top dog, for many years, was very quick; this was helped by the fact that Poodles do not shed their coats which enables them to be trimmed in many styles. In turn, this made them a fashionable breed to own and resulted in many poor specimens appearing which fell well short of the ideals of serious breeders. The cost of trimming the coat is the only drawback as, in every other way, the Poodle can be thoroughly recommended and is guaranteed to please – do ensure, especially in Miniatures and Toys, that the breeder is reputable. Alternatives – there is nothing quite like a Poodle, but the Bedlington Terrier does not shed its coat and the Bichon Frisé and the more unusual Löwchen will, no doubt, continue to gain in numbers.

SMALL BREEDS

Boston Terrier USA 36·8 cm. (14·5 in.) 7·8 kg. (17 lbs)

The national dog of the USA, this delightful breed is well recommended as a family pet. The short coat requires little grooming and is brindle or black with well defined white areas. Although small, the Boston has lost none of its fighting ancestry – it was developed from Bulldog × Terrier matings – so bigger dogs pick on it at their peril! Although well suited to apartment life, it is very active and needs plenty of exercise. The breed does not enjoy the sort of popularity it deserves and no doubt ardent breeders view this as a distinct blessing. Alternatives would be the larger French Bulldog or the Miniature Bull Terrier.

Cairn Terrier Scotland 30·5 cm. (10 in.) 6·4 kg. (14 lbs)

Bred for fox, badger and vermin hunting, the Cairn is a robust, lively and friendly little dog with typical Terrier pluck. His coat requires regular stripping to avoid being unsightly and matted, and the Cairn needs plenty of exercise if it is not to become overweight. They are reliable with young children and make excellent companions. Alternatives would be any of the small Terriers such as the West Highland White, Norwich, Norfolk, Scottish, or Border Terrier.

Cavalier King Charles Spaniel England 30·5 cm. (12 in.) 6·8 kg. (15 lbs)

These small Spaniels were very popular with royalty centuries ago but had virtually died out by Victorian times, following the growth of the flat-faced variety – the King Charles Spaniel. Since the revival of the breed, around 1930, Cavaliers have steadily increased in numbers to the point that they are now Britain's most popular Toy breed and are gaining ground every year in the USA. This is not surprising for they are cheerful, gentle and hardy little dogs. Their coat needs only light grooming and, unlike most Spaniels, does not need stripping. Their upkeep is thus well suited to today's economy. Similar is the King Charles, whilst an alternative breed would be the Papillon.

Pug

Chihuahua   Mexico   15·2 cm. (6 in.)   1·9 kg. (4 lbs)

The smallest dog in the world, the Chihuahua may be long or short-coated, the former being somewhat larger. They are perky little dogs with Terrier-like dispositions who just do not realize they are so small! Watch one 'attack' an over-inquisitive German Shepherd and you will know what I mean. Their handy size, minimal grooming and economic feeding makes them an ideal pet – how many other breeds could you pop in your handbag! Contrary to what might be thought, many men find these to be charming dogs to own. The very small ones are prone to lameness as a result of the knee-cap, or patella, moving abnormally, faulty dentition and running eyes, so choose with care. Alternatives would be the Miniature Pinscher, Papillon, and English Toy Terrier.

Dachshund   Germany   8·2 kg. (18 lbs)

Known as the *Teckel* in its homeland, the Dachshund may be seen in numerous forms; Standard and Miniature, Long-haired, Smooth, or Wire-haired – so there is plenty of choice. Affectionately called 'sausage dogs' by the layman, they are popular the world over. Grooming is minimal though it needs to be regular with the Long-haired variety. They are economic feeders, lively and strong as befits a breed developed to tackle badgers. They have friendly dispositions and their singular problem is that they are susceptible to intervertebral disk problems. The use of a harness, rather than a collar, is recommended when exercising them. They also enjoy digging which, whilst being discouraged by owners, is a natural thing for them to do. Similar long-backed breeds, though larger and more heavily coated, are Dandie Dinmont Terriers and Welsh Corgis.

Pekingese   China   20cm. (8in.)   4kg. (9lbs – bitches heavier)

Few breeds have had to accept the change from royal to popular pet to quite the same degree as the Pekingese, or Dragon or Lion Dog, has. For centuries only the Chinese Emperors could own these dogs which were accorded great rank and never allowed out of the Forbidden City. To steal, or even harm, one was punishable by death – such esteem were they held in. Following the British invasion of China during the last century, and capture of the Summer Palace, a number were exported to the UK and from that time onwards the breed just grew and grew in numbers. In spite of its more humble homes these days, the breed retains its air of majesty, its royal stubbornness and its loyalty to its master. Quite fearless, they make ideal apartment dogs but their profuse coats must be groomed very regularly. They become somewhat breathless in very hot weather and their eyes are prone to problems, so they need a lot of personal attention which most owners are more than pleased to bestow on them. Delightful little dogs. Similar in character, but more active, are Pugs and Griffons whilst the Tibetan Spaniel is another alternative. Surprisingly, the Peke's Japanese counterpart – the Japanese Chin, has not enjoyed the same success, but is certainly worthy of consideration before a purchase is made.

Shetland Sheepdog   Scotland   49·8cm. (14in.)   8·2kg. (18lbs)

Looking very much like a miniature Rough-haired Collie, the 'Sheltie' is in fact a separate breed, though it is likely there is some common origin between the breeds. A popular family dog, they are alert, energetic and intelligent. They dislike noise and do not respond to harsh treatment. They will need daily grooming if their dense coat is to be kept tangle free. They are highly trainable – as are all Collie breeds.

Dandie Dinmont Terrier

Shih Tzu   Tibet   24·1cm. (9·5in.)   6·4kg. (14lbs)

Pronounced *sheed-zoo* the breed, like many from the Orient, enjoyed a relatively luxurious life within the homes of the nobility. They are somewhat more outgoing than their Chinese cousins and this has helped them to gain great popularity in recent years, both in the UK and the USA. Their long coats will need plenty of attention but otherwise they exhibit less exaggeration than Pekes and are thus less prone to ailments – a further aid to their rise in numbers. Like all small oriental breeds they are ideal for apartments and were never bred to go on long walks as were many other breeds. The immediate alternative to the breed would be the Lhasa Apso or, for those with more time to spend on grooming, the all white Maltese.

Welsh Corgi   Wales   27·9cm. (11in.)   10kg. (22lbs)

There are two varieties of Corgi and the Pembroke is the more popular by far. Its cousin, the Cardigan, is easily recognized as it has a tail whereas the Pembroke does not, and the former is usually a little larger. This little Welsh cattle dog, or heeler, has been around for many centuries as a hard-working farm dog. However, when the Royal family acquired some and they were seen with the Queen, both in her palace and when on visits, the breed suddenly became a household pet, almost overnight. Few breeds have enjoyed the Corgi's level of press coverage over the years. They are easy to look after, require little grooming, are very hardy indeed and very lively, thus making them ideal pets. Temperament is more reliable in the Cardigan variety which never reached the dizzy heights of the Pembroke, and suffered less from irresponsible breeding as a result. No longer the top dog it was, the kindly nature of the Pembroke is now returning – thanks to its ardent breeder/supporters.

Pembroke
Welsh Corgi

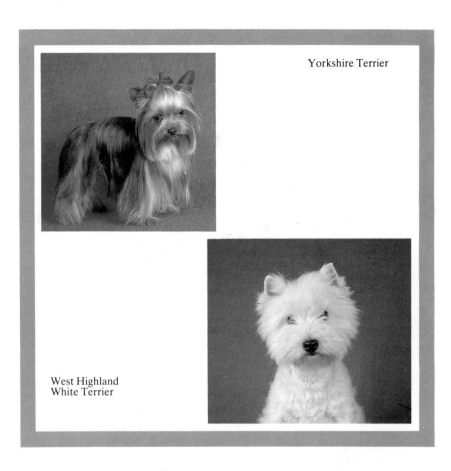

Yorkshire Terrier

West Highland
White Terrier

West Highland White Terrier   Scotland   27·9cm. (11 in.)   7kg. (15 lbs)

The most popular of the Terrier breeds, the 'Westie' has much to recommend it. They are very appealing with their white coats, cheerful, fun-loving and generally of a calmer nature than is normally associated with this group of breeds. The coarse coat will require trimming but otherwise the breed has no drawbacks, being easy to feed and undemanding in its exercise needs. The alternatives are the many Terriers available (*see under* Cairn).

Yorkshire Terrier   England   17·8cm. (7 in.)   2·8kg. (6 lbs)

One of the smallest dogs in the world, the 'Yorkie' is today very popular indeed. Economical to feed, easy to exercise and chirpy in nature, his drawback is that he will need grooming daily. This apart, he is an ideal lap dog. If young children are around, it is not recommended that a Yorkie be a family dog; they are very tiny and easily injured unintentionally. Alternatives would be Chihuahuas, Miniature Pinschers, English Toy Terriers, or, if you do not mind the grooming, the Pomeranian.

Breeds at a Glance

The list below will give the reader an idea of the many breeds that can be obtained. Further information on specific breeds should be acquired before the purchase of a given breed.

Abbreviations used are as follows: **Size:** S – Small; M – Medium; L – Large. **Coat:** S – Short or Smooth; M – Medium; MD – Medium to Long and Dense; L – Long; LD – Long and Dense.

	Size	Coat
GUNDOGS		
Britanny Spaniel	L	M
Drentse Partridge Dog	L	M
English Setter	L	M
German Longhaired Pointer	L	M
German Shorthaired Pointer	L	S
German Wirehaired pointer	L	M
Gordon Setter	L	M
Hungarian Vizsla	L	S
Irish Setter	L	S
Large Munsterlander	L	M
Pointer	L	S
Retriever (Chesapeake Bay)	L	M
Retriever (Curly Coated)	L	M
Retriever (Flat Coated)	L	M
Retriever (Golden)	L	M
Retriever (Labrador)	L	S
Spaniel (American Cocker)	M	MD
Spaniel (American Water)	M	MD
Spaniel (Clumber)	M	MD
Spaniel (Cocker)	M	M
Spaniel (English Springer)	M	M
Spaniel (Field)	M	M
Spaniel (Irish Water)	M	MD
Spaniel (Sussex)	M	M
Spaniel (Welsh Springer)	M	M
Weimaraner	L	S
HOUNDS		
Afghan	L	L
Basenji	M	S
Basset	M	S
Beagle	M	S
Bloodhound	L	S
Borzoi	L	MD
Coonhound (Black & Tan)	L	S
Dachshund (Long-haired)	S	L
Dachshund (Miniature Long)	S	L
Dachshund (Smooth)	S	S
Dachshund (Miniature Smooth)	S	S
Dachshund (Wire)	S	S
Dachshund (Miniature Wire)	S	S
Deerhound	L	M
Elkhound (Norwegian)	M	MD
Finnish Spitz	M	M
Foxhound (American)	L	S
Foxhound (English)	M	S

	Size	Coat
HOUNDS Cont.		
Greyhound	L	S
Harrier	M	S
Ibizan	L	S
Irish Wolfhound	L	M
Otterhound	L	M
Pharaoh Hound	L	S
Portuguese Warren Hound	L	S
Rhodesian Ridgeback	L	S
Saluki	L	S
Sloughi (Algerian Greyhound)	L	S
Whippet	S	S
TERRIERS		
Airedale Terrier	L	MD
Australian Terrier	S	MD
Bedlington Terrier	M	MD
Border Terrier	S	MD
Bull Terrier	M	S
Bull Terrier (Miniature)	S	S
Cairn Terrier	S	MD
Dandie Dinmont Terrier	S	MD
Fox Terrier (Smooth)	M	S
Fox Terrier (Wire)	M	MD
Glen of Imaal Terrier	S	MD
Irish Terrier	M	MD
Kerry Blue Terrier	M	MD
Lakeland Terrier	M	MD
Manchester Terrier	S	S
Norfolk Terrier	S	MD
Norwich Terrier	S	MD
Scottish Terrier	S	MD
Sealyham Terrier	S	MD
Skye Terrier	S	LD
Soft-Coated Wheaten Terrier	M	LD
Staffordshire Bull Terrier	M	S
Welsh Terrier	M	MD
West Highland White Terrier	S	MD

WORKING	Size	Coat
Alaskan Malamute	L	MD
Anatolian (Karabash) Dog	L	MD
Bearded Collie	M	L
Belgian Shepherd (Groenendael)	L	M
Belgian Shepherd (Lackenois)	L	M
Belgian Shepherd (Malinois)	L	M
Belgian Shepherd (Tervueren)	L	M
Bernese Mountain Dog	L	MD
Border Collie	M	M
Bouvier Des Flandres	L	MD
Boxer	L	S
Briard	L	L
Bullmastiff	L	S
Collie (Rough)	L	MD
Collie (Smooth)	L	S
Dobermann	L	S
Eskimo Dog	M	MD
Estrela Mountain Dog	L	MD
German Shepherd (Alsatian)	L	M
Great Dane	L	S
Hungarian Kuvasz	L	MD
Hungarian Puli	L	MD
Komondor	L	LD
Maremma Sheepdog	L	MD
Mastiff	L	S
Neopolitan Mastiff	L	S
Newfoundland	L	MD
Norwegian Buhund	M	MD
Old English Sheepdog	L	LD
Pyrenean Mountain Dog	L	MD
Rottweiler	L	S
St Bernard	L	MD
Samoyed	L	MD
Shetland Sheepdog	S	MD
Siberian Husky	L	MD
Swedish Vallhund	S	S
Welsh Corgi (Cardigan)	S	S
Welsh Corgi (Pembroke)	S	S

UTILITY (Non-Sporting in USA)	Size	Coat
Boston Terrier	S	S
Bulldog	M	S
Caanan Dog	M	M
Chow Chow	M	MD
Dalmatian	L	S
French Bulldog	M	S
Giant Schnauzer	L	LD
Iceland Dog	M	MD
Japanese Spitz	M	MD
Keeshond	M	LD
Leonberger	L	MD
Lhasa Apso	S	LD
Miniature Schnauzer	S	MD
Poodle (Miniature)	S–M	MD
Poodle (Standard)	L	MD
Poodle (Toy)	S	MD

TOY	Size	Coat
Affenpinscher	S	S
Australian Silky Terrier	S	L
Bichon Frise	S	MD
Cavalier King Charles Spaniel	S	S
Chihuahua (Long-Coat)	S	M
Chihuahua (Smooth-Coat)	S	S
Chinese Crested	S	S
English Toy Terrier (Black & Tan)	S	S
Griffon Bruxellois	S	S
Italian Greyhound	S	S

TOY Cont.	Size	Coat
Japanese Chin	S	M
King Charles Spaniel	S	M
Lowchen	S	M
Maltese	S	L
Miniature Pinscher	S	S
Papillon	S	S
Pekingese	S	MD
Pomeranian	S	MD
Pug	S	S
Schipperke	S	M
Schnauzer	S	M
Shih Tzu	S	LD
Tibetan Apso	S	MD
Tibetan Spaniel	S	MD
Tibetan Terrier	S	MD
Yorkshire Terrier	S	L

MISCELLANEOUS BREEDS

The following breeds, whilst seen, are not officially recognised by either the American or British Kennel Clubs.

Akita Inu	L	MD
Australian Heeler	M	M
Australian Kelpie	M	M
Jack Russell Terrier	S	S–M
Mexican Hairless	S	S
Portuguese Podengo	S–L	S
Spinoni Italiani	L	S

RECOMMENDED FURTHER READING COVERING ALL BREEDS

The Complete Dog Book, The American Kennel Club, Howell Book House, New York.

The Dog Owner's Home Veterinary Handbook, D. G. Carlson, DVM & J. Giffin, MD, Howell Book House, New York

Kennel Club Addresses

American Kennel Club
51 Madison Avenue
New York
N.Y. 10010, USA

Australian Kennel Club
Royal Show Grounds
Ascot Vale
Victoria
Australia

The Kennel Club
1 Clarges Street
Piccadilly
London, W.1.
England

Barbados Kennel Club
Wraysbury
Bucks, St Thomas
Barbados
West Indies

Bermuda Kennel Club Inc.
PO Box 1455
Hamilton 5
Bermuda

Canadian Kennel Club,
2150 Bloor Street West
Toronto M6S 1M8
Ontario
Canada

Kennel Club of India
Kenhope, Coonoor 1
Nilgiris
S. India

Irish Kennel Club
23 Earlsfort Terrace
Dublin 2
Eire

Jamaican Kennel Club
8 Orchard Street
Kingston 5
Jamaica
West Indies

Malaysian Kennel Association
PO Box 559
Kuala Lumpur
Malaya

Malta Kennel Club
1 Simon Flats
Dr Zammit Street
Balzan
Malta GC

New Zealand Kennel Club
PO Box 19
101 Aro Street
Wellington
New Zealand

The Singapore Kennel Club
275f Selegie Complex
Selegie Road
Singapore 7

Kennel Union of Southern Africa
6th Floor, Bree Castle
68 Bree Street
Cape Town 8001
South Africa

A beautiful study of the Maremma
Sheepdog – for those who like something
different.

My Dog's Information Page

Kennel Club Name: _____

No. _____   _____

Pet Name: _____ Sex: _____

Color: _____ Date of Birth: _____

Sire: _____

Dam: _____

Breeder: _____

_____

Date Purchased: _____ Identity No. _____

Vaccinations Given: _____

Date: _____ Boosters Due: _____

Useful Telephone Numbers

Breeder: _____ Veterinarian: _____

Boarding Kennel: _____ Kennel Club: _____

Training Class: _____ Pet Store: _____

Police/Dog Pound: _____